MUSIC COMPOSED BY **ALEXANDRE DESPLAT**
ORIGINAL MOTION PICTURE SOUNDTRACK

ILLUMINATION PRESENTS

THE SECRET LIFE OF **Pets**™

HAL•LEONARD®
7777 W. BLUEMOUND RD. P.O. BOX 13819 MILWAUKEE, WI 53213

ISBN 978-1-4950-7465-3
Visit Hal Leonard Online at **www.halleonard.com**

MEET THE PETS

By ALEXANDRE DESPLAT

KATIE'S LEAVING

By ALEXANDRE DESPLAT

ME LIKE WHAT ME SEE

By ALEXANDRE DESPLAT

TELENOVELA SQUIRRELS

By ALEXANDRE DESPLAT

ME LIKE WHAT ME SEE

By ALEXANDRE DESPLAT

MEET DUKE

By ALEXANDRE DESPLAT

TELENOVELA SQUIRRELS

By ALEXANDRE DESPLAT

ROOFTOP ROUTE

By ALEXANDRE DESPLAT

Cool Swing

With pedal

YOU HAVE AN OWNER?

By ALEXANDRE DESPLAT

Slowly, with freedom

GOOD MORNING MAX

By ALEXANDRE DESPLAT

SEWER CHASE

By ALEXANDRE DESPLAT

WET BUT HANDSOME/BLUE TAXI

By ALEXANDRE DESPLAT

Rock 'n' Roll Shuffle

MAX AND GIDGET

By ALEXANDRE DESPLAT

WELCOME HOME

By ALEXANDRE DESPLAT

WE GO TOGETHER

Lyric and Music by WARREN CASEY
and JIM JACOBS

TRAVELING BOSSA

By ALEXANDRE DESPLAT